CIRCU[LAR]

PEAK DI[STRICT]
AIRCRAFT WRECKS

by
John D. Mason

Photographs by C.M.Mason.
Maps by John N. Merrill.

TRAIL CREST PUBLICATIONS

1992

CIRCULAR WALKS by JOHN N. MERRILL

ACKNOWLEDGEMENTS

My wife, her enthusiasm and boundless energy in completing these walks in all weather conditions, and her love of photography.

Ralph Hoon, former Pilot Officer of 460 Pathfinder Squadron, R.A.A.F. Binbrook (Royal Australian Air Force) and Flight Lieutenant of 90 Squadron, Photo Reconnaissance, R.A.F.

Fellow ramblers, and crash site explorers - Geoff Hibberd of Sheffield and Geoff Young of Derby.

M.O.D. Air Historical Branch. R.A.F. London.

M.O.D. Accident Records. London.

Numerous Aviation books and manuals, including - R.Collier's and D.J.Smith's books on aircraft wrecks.

*Piece of undercarriage leg from Harvard, crashed 14.1.52
below Woolpacks - Walk No. 5*

TRAIL CREST
PUBLICATIONS
Ltd.,
WINSTER,
MATLOCK,
DERBYSHIRE.
DE4 2DQ
 Winster (0629) 650454
Winster (0629) 650416

Edited, typeset, designed, paged, marketed and distributed
by John N. Merrill.

© Text and routes - John D.Mason 1992.
© Maps - John N. Merrill 1992.
© Photographs - C.M.Mason 1992.

First Published - September 1991
Reprinted May 1992
ISBN 0 907496 94 6

Please note : The maps in this guide are purely illustrative. You are encouraged to walk with the appropriate Ordnance Survey map as detailed for each walk.

Meticulous research has been undertaken to ensure that this publication is highly accurate at the time of going to press. The publishers, however, cannot be held responsible for alterations, errors or omissions, but they would welcome notification of such for future editions.

Typeset in - Palatino - bold, italic and plain 9pt and 18pt.

Printed by - John N. Merrill at Milne House, Speedwell Mill, Miller's Green, Wirksworth, Derbyshire. DE4 4BL

Cover photograph - Meteors wreckages - see Walk 2.
© C.M.Mason1992.

An all British product.

CONTENTS

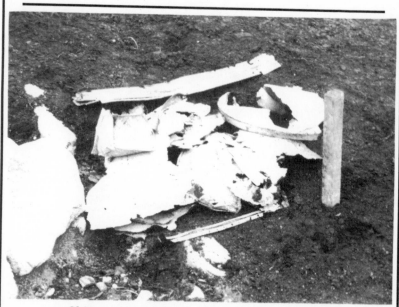

About the author....

John Mason was born in Mablethorpe, Lincolnshire in 1947 and is married with no children. He has been living and working in the Derby area for a number of years. His interest in hill walking began as a schoolboy with the ascent of Snowdon. He enjoys the hills of Wales, the Lake District and Peak District. He plans to visit and log all the many aircraft crash sites scattered over the mountainous regions of Britain.

The author at the Wellington Bomber X3348 crash site - 26.1.43 Blackden Edge, Kinder Scout. The photograph is taken 150 yards S.E. of O.S. pillar on Blackden Edge.

Chipmunk remains on Arnfield Moor - Walk 8.

INTRODUCTION

All the walks are covered by the Ordnance Survey Outdoor Leisure Map - **The Dark Peak.**

To complete these walks, a basic knowledge of map reading and compass work is essential. Owing to the isolation of a number of the crash sites, weather conditions must always be taken into consideration. A blanket of snow for example will cover some of the smaller sites. The hills and moorlands must always be treated with respect, as weather conditions can change dramatically within minutes.

All wreckage at the crash sites is crown property and M.O.D. permission is required for any removal. A number of larger parts, notably engines, have been recovered and placed in R.A.F. Museums. Removal by members of the public is totally pointless, as eventually, there will be nothing of any significance for enthusiasts to look for. The sites should also be considered as memorials to the brave air crews, many of whom perished in the Dark Peak.

Sabre ruins - crashed 18.12.54 - Great Hill, Holme Moss - Walk No. 2.

WALK 1
DOVESTONES & CHEW AREA

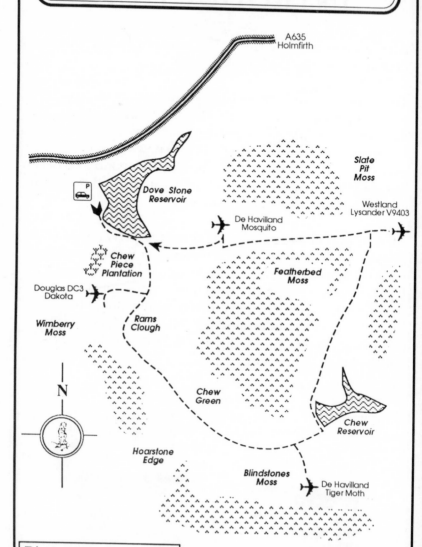

A635
Holmfirth

Slate
Pit
Moss

Dove Stone
Reservoir

Westland
Lysander V9403

De Havilland
Mosquito

Chew
Piece
Plantation

Featherbed
Moss

Douglas DC3
Dakota

Wimberry
Moss

Rams
Clough

N

Chew
Green

Chew
Reservoir

Hoarstone
Edge

Blindstones
Moss

De Havilland
Tiger Moth

Distance - approx. 7 miles.

Walk 1

- DOVESTONES & CHEW AREA

- Allow 5 hours for the walk.

 at Dovestone Reservoir. Grid reference 103036

Dovestone Reservoir - Chew Brook - Chew Piece Plantation - Wimberry Stones - Rams Clough - Chew Green - Chew Hurdles - Blindstones Moss - Chew Reservoir - Slate Pit Moss- Dovestone Moss - Dove Stones - Dovestone Reservoir.

WALKING NOTES - *There are toilet facilities and a part time Peak Park Ranger and Information Service at the reservoir.*
The Douglas Dakota on Wimberry Stones, and the ridge walk from the top of Rams Clough to Chew Hurdles, is on private land, owned by The Stalybridge Estates; from whom permission should be requested before entering their land.

WALKING INSTRUCTIONS - From the car park, walk along the road southwards around the reservoir, passing the sailing club. Go through the metal gate, and just before the footbridge crossing Chew Brook, go right through a gap in the wall, and follow the path beside Chew Brook until you reach the start of Rams Clough, passing a weir, and turning right on reaching a giant boulder. Follow the path running alongside the fence and trees to a stile, do not cross the stile, keep straight on following the fence, with the Wimberry Stones rocky heights directly above you. As you reach the corner of the fencing, next to a single tree, cross the broken wall, and continue along with the wall and fence on your right, until you reach the end of Chew Piece Plantation, where you will arrive at another fence and gate. This land is owned by The Stalybridge Estates. Go through the gate, and after a few metres turn left, there you will find the propeller reduction gear off a Pratt and Whitney engine, from the DC3 Dakota, it lies at the bottom of a rocky watercourse which runs to the top of Wimberry Stones.

Head up the watercourse for approx 150 metres, where you will find a square section of undercarriage leg, sadly, this and the reduction gear are the only notable remains of the Dakota. The actual crash site is near the top of the watercourse, if you decide to explore higher up, you will find a few pieces of molten metal fused to the rocks. After your inspection of the area, retrace your steps back to the single tree at the corner of Chew Piece Plantation. Here turn right and head up Rams Clough. (Alternatively, you may decide to walk on the lower route to Chew Reservoir, if you wish to travel on this route, retrace your steps back to the metalled road at Dovestone Reservoir, and follow the road south easterly all the way up to Chew. At the southern corner of the reservoir, pick up the path going westerly for about 200 metres until you reach the access point.) If you take the route up Rams Clough, you will find it a steep climb and very rocky in places, it can also be very slippery when wet, so care must be taken, at the top of the clough, turn left and follow the ridge east-wards, there is a path of sorts, it becomes rather indistinct at times, but the way is quite safe. Follow the ridge as it contours around Chew Green and Chew Hurdles, passing a white marker post and crossing a small stream. The path does become clearer, and eventually you will reach an access point approx 200 metres before Chew Reservoir.

Here turn right and head up a distinct gully next to the access point, after approx 75 metres, the gully branches left and right, go right for about another 75 metres and climb out of the gully on the right hand side, here in a small peaty hollow you will find the remains of the De Havilland Tiger Moth. Just a few rusty engine bearer struts, scraps of twisted metal, and part of the sump from the Gypsy Major Engine and pieces of wood, are all that remain at the site.

After your exploration of the site, head for Chew Reservoir, and on reaching it, follow the wall on it's western side. At the end of the wall, take a compass bearing of 22° and head northwards to the high ground on Slate Pit Moss. The ground is very boggy in places, especially in winter, and you will have to traverse quite a number of peat gullies and watercourses. Approx 30 minutes walking will bring you to a marker post on the highest point of Featherbed Moss. It is the first post of a line running along Featherbed Moss to Slate Pit Moss. At the post turn right heading east, you will see Holme Moss Mast in the distance. About 200 metres from the post, you will find the crash site of the Westland Lysander. There isn't much of the plane left to examine, just a few scraps of metal and wood lying near a stream outlet, some parts are probably buried under the peat.

After your inspection, set your compass to 272° and head westerly, first to the marker post, then across Featherbed Moss and Dovestone Moss, eventually reaching the summit of Dove Stones. Here you have a magnificent view of the reservoir. From your lofty vantage point, you will see a broken wall running down towards the reservoir, follow the wall down for approx 200 metres, and where the rocky ground turns grassy, turn right and walk for another 100 metres northwards, until you reach a grassy plateau. The remains of the De Havilland Mosquito lie on the plateau, in the lee of a rocky slope. Only a few pieces of this majestic night fighter are left. Pieces of heavily rusted tubular framework, three pieces of armour plating, and scraps of molten metal. After your investigation of the site, head down the steep slope to the reservoir, where you will pick up the path back to your car park.

WRECKS SEEN ON THIS WALK -

Douglas DC3 Dakota
G-AHCY B.E.A.

Crashed Wimberry Stones 19.8.49
Grid reference - 015026 - 015027

De Havilland Tiger Moth

Crashed Blindstones Moss
12.4.45 Grid reference - 035016

Westland Lysander V9403
of 6 AA C.U.

Crashed Slate Pit Moss 19.8.41
Grid reference - 041033

De Havilland Mosquito
PF 395 571 Sqdn R.A.F.

Crashed Dean Rocks / Dove Stones
22.10.44 Grid Reference - 024033

Dakota undercarriage - crashed 19.8.49 - Wimberry Stones.

Dakota propellor reduction gear - crashed 19.8.49 - Wimberry Stones.

Armour plating from Mosquito - Crashed 22.10.44, Dean Rocks.

Tiger Moth wreckage - crashed 12.4.45 - Near Chew Reservoir.

WALK 2
HOLME MOSS

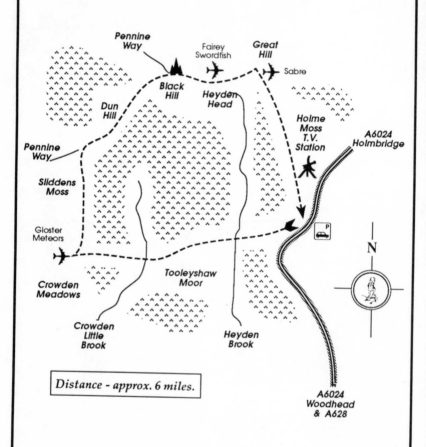

Pennine Way

Fairey Swordfish

Great Hill

Sabre

Black Hill

Heyden Head

Dun Hill

Holme Moss T.V. Station

Pennine Way

A6024 Holmbridge

Sliddens Moss

Gloster Meteors

P

N

Crowden Meadows

Tooleyshaw Moor

Crowden Little Brook

Heyden Brook

A6024 Woodhead & A628

Distance - approx. 6 miles.

Walk 2
HOLME MOSS
- allow 4 to 5 hours.

🚗 *- off the road, on the A6024 Holmfirth Road, just below the Holme Moss Transmitter on Wilmer Hill. Grid Reference 096037*

👣 👣 👣 *- Holme Moss, Wilmer Hill, Heyden Brook, Tooleyshaw Moor, Crowden Meadows, Sliddens Moss, Pennine Way, Dun Hill, Black Hill, Trig Point, Heyden Head, Great Hill, Holme Moss .*

WALKING NOTES - *Holme Moss Mast is a 750ft B.B.C. Television Transmitter. Allow 4-5 hours for the walk, preferably on a clear day.*

WALKING INSTRUCTIONS - The access to open country is next to the parking area, from here set your compass to 260° west, and set off down the hillside, following a grassy water course with the sheepfold on your left. On reaching the bottom, cross Heyden Brook, with the disused quarries to your right, and climb up the opposite hillside, following a rough track part of the way up. On reaching the summit, cross the path that runs along the top of Tooleyshaw Moor, this path leads to Black Hill. Keeping on your compass bearing, go down the hill and cross another brook, beware of low flying aircraft on their way to Manchester Airport, this area must be part of the flight path. Rabbits are in abundance on these moors, they often startle you, as they come running out of their burrows or grazing places. A stone hut can be seen a few hundred metres to your left, on Crowden Meadows, and you pass a rocky outcrop on the right, this is marked on the O.S. map.

The ground is quite boggy in places as you cross Sliddens Moss, so care should be taken. On a clear day, you should see part of the wreckage on the horizon. Carry on until you reach the crash site of the Gloster Meteors. The wreckage is strewn over quite a large area, starting from the head of Meadow Clough, some pieces are in peat gullies, including an engine casing, undercarriage and wing pieces, one numbered 365903. There are numerous other sections dotted about the area.

After your inspection, and a well earned rest, head due north, crossing the summit of Sliddens Moss, keeping Holme Moss Mast to your right, until you reach Meadowgrain Clough, and the Pennine Way. Here turn north-east and follow the Pennine Way up to Dun Hill, passing a large stone cairn, and on up to the trig point on Black Hill. The area is a mass of treacherous peat in wet weather, so be prepared for the worst. At the trig point, take a compass bearing of 90° east, the mast should be in front and slightly to your right, cross over the peat groughs, and after approx 10 minutes, you will come to a fairly wide peat gully just before the top of Heyden Head. The wreckage of the Fairey Swordfish lies in the bottom of the gully, pieces of twisted metal, very rusted tubular frame work, and other fragments. Sadly this is all that remains, though probably some parts have sunk into the clinging peat. The Henlow R.A.F. cadets recovered the nine-cylinder Bristol Pegasus 750 HP engine, and presented it to the Royal Navy Aircraft Museum in 1968.

Now set your compass to 78° and head easterly, keeping the mast to your right, scramble across the peat gullies towards Great Hill, passing a small concrete Boundary Post. After approx 10 minutes, you will arrive at the crash site of the F86. Sabre, on a large grassy area between flat peat beds.

Parts of undercarriage and wings are left, some with numbers on them, though they are hardly legible, there are other fragments of metal scattered about the peat beds, which are worth exploring in dry weather. Directly ahead of you are the villages of Holme, and Holmebridge, surrounded by hills. After your inspection head towards the mast, if it's a misty day and you cannot see the mast, set your compass to 160° and head south, crossing more peat gullies and flat beds, then onto the grassy area of Holme Moss. After a few minutes you will reach the boundary fencing of the Transmitter, which you skirt round to reach the road and your parking area.

WRECKS SEEN ON THIS WALK -

Gloster Meteors *W.A. 971 V.Z. 518* *66 Sqdn R.A.F.*	*Crashed Sliddens Moss. Crowden* *Meadows. 12.4.51* *Grid reference- 069029*
Fairey Swordfish *P4223* *751 Sqdn Fleet Air Arm*	*Crashed Heyden Head 25.1.40* *Grid Reference - 0845047*
North American *F.86 E. Sabre* *19234 137 T. Flight R.C.A.F.*	*Crashed Great Hill 18.12.54* *Grid Reference - 091050*

Meteors wreckage - Crashed 12.4.51 - Sliddens Moss.

Swordfish wreckage - crashed 25.1.40 - Heydon Head, Holme Moss.

WALK 3
HIGHER SHELF STONES

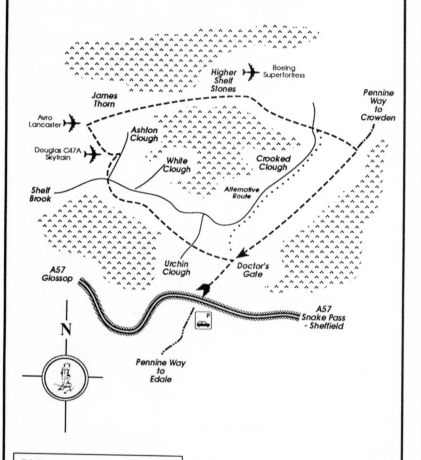

Distance - approx. 5 miles.

Walk 3
HIGHER SHELF STONES
-allow 4 hours

 - On the Snake Road summit where the Pennine Way crosses the A57. Grid reference 088929.

A57 Snake Road, Pennine Way, Doctors Gate, Ashton Clough, James Thorn, Lower Shelf Stones, Higher Shelf Stones, Trig point, Alport Low, Crooked Clough, Doctors Gate, Pennine Way, A57 Snake Road.

WALKING NOTES *-This is a fairly short, though very interesting walk, best attempted on a clear day. Allow 4 hours.*

WALKING INSTRUCTIONS - Proceed northwards along the Pennine Way, crossing a stile at the wooden gate. After approx 250 metres you will reach the track known as Doctors Gate, believed to be a classical example of a medieval packhorse (gate) road, linking Glossop and Brough. The road was named after Dr. John Talbot, vicar of Glossop between 1494 - 1550. He is believed to be responsible for making the rough track more accessible for traders, by improving the surface.

On reaching the track, turn left as signposted for Glossop and follow it as it meanders down, quite steeply in places, crossing the stream running through "Urchin Clough" which can dry up in the summer. The track becomes very rocky, and you will then cross another stream running through "Rose Clough". Further down, across Shelf Brook you will see the entrance to "White Clough" and not far past it "Ashton Clough", which is your destination. Two trees at the entrance of the clough will help you identify it. To reach it, you will have to come down off the track, veer right, and cross Shelf Brook. On reaching the trees, follow the stream bed up the clough, it is very rocky and quite steep in places, so care should be taken. After approx 10 minutes, you will find the first piece of the Douglas C47A Skytrain in the stream bed, an engine and piece of undercarriage leg. Carry on up the clough, over the rocky cascades, where you will see part of an engine, though it can easily be missed if the stream is in full flow.

Further up the clough lies the second engine, the huge plane was powered by 14 cylinder twin wasp radial engines, manufactured by Pratt and Whitney. Nearby lies a wheel with rusty undercarriage struts and pieces of fuselage, a little higher up is the largest piece of wreckage in the clough, slowly being buried under the rocks and soil, from this last section of wreckage, proceed up out of the clough on the left hand bank, heading northwards, after a few minutes you will come to a section of undercarriage on the hillside, there are pieces of wing and fuselage nearby. Carry on up the hill north westerly, and you will find more shattered pieces of wing and fuselage, the majority being in three shallow hollows, there are many more pieces scattered around the area.

From the crash site you have a fine view of the northern edges of the Kinder massif way over to the south, and the Snake road with 'Doctors Gate' track far below you. Now set your compass to 297° and head up the slope in a westerly direction, after a few minutes you will come to the crash site of the Avro Lancaster. It lies just below the summit of James Thorn, a few feet higher and this famous old bomber would have cleared the hill, the plane must have exploded in a ball of flame, as most of the remaims are molten metal, distorted into shapeless lumps, a few pieces of reinforcing struts and other fragments are scattered about the area.

After your inspection, set your compass to 100° and head in an easterly direction towards Lower Shelf Stones, the rocky outcrop is easily distinguishable on a clear day. You will cross a tract of peat, then a rocky area, and onto a mossy stretch running up to the brow of Lower Shelf Stones. Carry on, crossing another stretch of peat until you reach the next mass of rocks, these are Higher Shelf Stones with a trig point in the middle of them. From the trig point, walk 64° east for five minutes, you will arrive in the centre of the crash site of the Boeing B29 Superfortress, the largest crash site in the Dark Peak area.

There are four 18 cylinder Wright cyclone radial engines, large wing and fuselage sections, pieces of undercarriage, and masses of smaller pieces, all scattered around a large area below the trig point. A memorial plaque has been placed at the site, it was carried onto Higher Shelf Stones by a Sea King helicopter, and set into it's present location by members of the R.A.F. The site is presently used by the R.A.F. as an altimeter reading course. A wreath is laid at the site every year, probably by relatives of the American crew that so tragically perished here.

After your inspection, return to the trig point and head 120° east, towards Alport Low, crossing the grassy and rock strewn slopes of Higher Shelf Stones, and the mossy flats of Gathering Hill, eventually reaching the stream running through Crooked Clough, here you have a choice of routes back to your car, either carry on your compass bearing, following a water course where you will reach the Pennine Way in approx 20 minutes, upon where, you will turn right and follow the path back to the A57 or, turn right at Crooked Clough, and follow the stream bed, this route is more pleasant and picturesque than walking along the heavily trodden Pennine Way. The stream meanders down the narrow clough, cascading over a waterfall which you will have to scramble down the side of, eventually reaching another waterfall, which I find easier to cross from above on the left hand bank, from here stay on the higher ground, gradually working your way up the slope to Doctors Gate, where you will find a stone cairn, here turn left up the rocky path, and follow it eastwards back to the signpost, where you turn right along the short stretch of Pennine Way, and so back to your car.

WRECKS SEEN ON THIS WALK -

Douglas C47A Skytrain *Crashed on James Thorn 24.7.45*
42-108982/J 314 TCG   *Grid references- 0815946 0809475*

Avro Lancaster   *Crashed on James Thorn 18.5.45*
KB993/EQ-U 408 Sqdn *Grid reference- 077948*

Boeing RB-29A F13A   *Crashed Higher Shelf Stones*
Superfortress 44-61999   *3.11.48*
16th PR Sqdn   *Grid reference- 091949*
311th Air Division
named "Over Exposed"

*Superfortress - main undercarraige - crashed 3.11.48
Higher Shelf Stones, Bleaklow.*

*Superfortress - wing section - crashed 3.11.48
Higher Shelf Stones, Bleaklow.*

C47 Skytrain - part of Pratt and Whitney fourteen cylinder radial engine - crashed 27.7.45 - Ashton Clough, Bleaklow.

Lancaster wreckcage - crashed 18.5.45 - James Thorn.

WALK 4
ROUND HILL

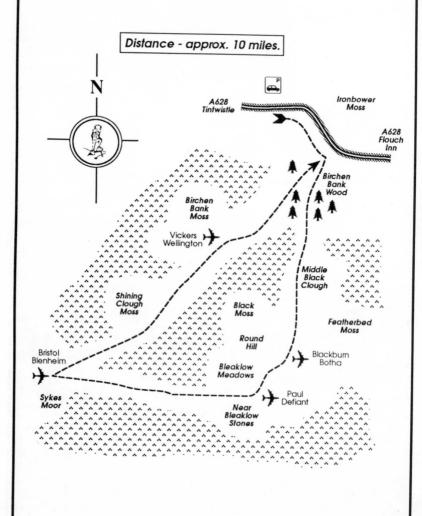

Distance - approx. 10 miles.

N

A628 Tintwistle

Ironbower Moss

A628 Flouch Inn

Birchen Bank Wood

Birchen Bank Moss

Vickers Wellington

Middle Black Clough

Shining Clough Moss

Black Moss

Round Hill

Featherbed Moss

Bristol Blenheim

Blackburn Botha

Bleaklow Meadows

Paul Defiant

Sykes Moor

Near Bleaklow Stones

Walk 4
- ROUND HILL
- Allow 6 hours

🚗 *Parking off the main A628 road, just past Woodhead Reservoir at the bottom of the slip road. Grid reference 114999*

👣 👣 👣 *A628 Slip Road, Birchen Bank Wood, Middle Black Clough, Round Hill, Near Bleaklow Stones, Sykes Moor, Shining Clough Moss, Stable Clough, Birchen Bank Moss, Near Black Clough, Birchen Bank Wood, Slip Road.*

WALKING NOTES - This is quite a long and fairly hard walk, though very picturesque and rewarding. Best attempted on a fine clear day.

WALKING INSTRUCTIONS - Cross the footbridge at the access point and follow the stream southwards, towards Birchen Bank Wood. Cross another stile next to a metal gate, and follow the track next to the stream, passing the green shooting cabins on your right. Birchen Bank Wood is very pretty, and full of birds and wildlife though it is best appreciated early in the morning, as it tends to attract a lot of people during the day. Cross the stream where it widens out, onto the left hand bank, and carry on through the trees. Where the stream branches left and right, take the left side going south-east, this is the start of Middle Black Clough. The frequent downpours that douse the Bleaklow plateau, ensure a constant flow of water down this delightful clough, so cross with care, you may choose to stay within the clough on the left side, where there is a path of sorts, or climb up to the rim and follow the path through the heather, along the left hand side of the clough.

I choose to stay within the clough, it is quite steep and rocky in places, and you will have to criss cross the stream bed a number of times to obtain the easiest route up. About an hours walking up the clough, will bring you to a distinct rocky watercourse running from the right, into the clough directly where the stream bed bends, adjacent to a grassy bank. Follow the watercourse upwards, going south west for approx

50 metres, then where it then forks left and right, take the right fork, going west for approx another 50 metres, and climb out of the stream bed onto the right hand bank. You will see in front of you, approx 100 metres away in a north-westerly direction, the remains of the Blackburn Botha, with Holme Moss Mast directly behind it. Two large heavy wing sections and pieces of fuselage are scattered around the crash site. There are other pieces of aluminium which tend to get blown around on a windy day.

You are now on Round Hill, to the north of you lies Black Hill, (very aptly named) and to the south Bleaklow Hill, which is your next port of call. Set your compass to 228° and head south/westerly across Bleaklow Meadows, towards the rocky area of 'Near Bleaklow Stones' Crossing a number of gullies, until you reach the slopes of Near Bleaklow Stones. As you go up, you will find wreckage of the Boulton Paul Defiant strewn along peat gullies, and at the top of a gully, in a flat clearing, you will find more wreckage including a 1260 HP Rolls Royce Merlin engine, and some undercarriage struts.

After your inspection set your compass to 279° , and head westerly along Shining Clough Moss, with the Pennine Way to your left, and above you. After a few minutes you will cross the stream bed running through near Black Clough, carry on your compass bearing, crossing numerous gullies. This is very hard walking and the gullies seem unrelenting, but eventually you will come to the flatter ground of Sykes Moor. As you reach the moor, you will see directly in front of you the upper reaches of Torside Clough, with the Pennine Way running up it's left flank. Your compass bearing should bring you to a small marker post, with a piece of flat aluminium attached to it. It is situated a few hundred metres east of Torside Clough. In a gully next to the marker post you will find a few scraps of twisted metal from the Bristol Blenheim. From here, walk northwards for approx 100 metres, and you will find a solitary Bristol Mercury engine in the heather, from the engine go east for another 110 metres, and you will find more of the wreckage in a gully, then walk a few more metres north to a larger gully and there you will find another engine, with large pieces of the shattered tail unit.

If you explore the vicinity, you will find countless parts of the wrecked plane in gullies and shallow clearings. The crash site covers a large area, I seem to find different pieces each time I visit the site. After your inspection, and well earned rest, proceed from the gully containing the engine and tail unit on a compass bearing of 54°, heading easterly towards Shining Clough Moss with Holme Moss mast on your left, after a few minutes you will come to a fence that has been pulled down in places, cross this and carry on your bearing crossing the dreaded gullies again, you will also cross some large water courses, notably the one running through Stable Clough, eventually, after about an hours slog, you should reach some posts on Birchen Bank Moss. If you look over to your left towards Black Hill, the road leading to Holme Moss mast can be seen, the crash site of the Vickers Wellington is in a line to the right of the road. It lies between two gullies on flat ground in the heather, near to two of the posts mentioned earlier. There is a small marker post with scraps of metal attached to it, which should help you find the site, as it can be difficult to locate especially in bad weather, but if you search around the area of the lower posts you will be successful. Sadly, only a few fragments of twisted metal from the large bomber remain, gathered in a pile next to the metal post, though there are fragments scattered around the area, if you wish to explore.

After your inspection, stay on the same compass bearing until you reach the track running along the top of Near Black Clough, go down the track northerly, taking in the pretty sight of the clough, which is most welcome after the hard walk across the moors. Follow the track past the trees, and down the slope onto the path where you started from, re-cross the stile next to the metal gate and on to the car parking area.

WRECKS SEEN ON THIS WALK -

Blackburn Botha
W5103 7FPP
Grid reference- 110974

Crashed Round Hill 10.12.41
Bleaklow

Boulton Paul Defiant
N.3378 255 Sqdn.
Grid reference- 106970

Crashed Near Bleaklow
Stones 29.8.41

Bristol Blenheim
L 1476 64 Sqdn.

Crashed Sykes Moor 30.1.39
Grid reference- 0815971

Vickers Wellington
R 1011 28 OTU.
Grid reference- 105986

Crashed Birchen Bank
Moss 30.1.43

Botha W5103 wreckage - crashed 10.12.41 - Round Hill.

Defiant wreckage - crashed 29.8.41 - Near Bleaklow Stones.

Blenheim wreckage - crashed 30.1.39 - Sykes Moor, Bleaklow.

Wellington wreckage - crashed 30.1.43 - Birchen Bank Moss, Bleaklow,

WALK 5
BROWN KNOLL

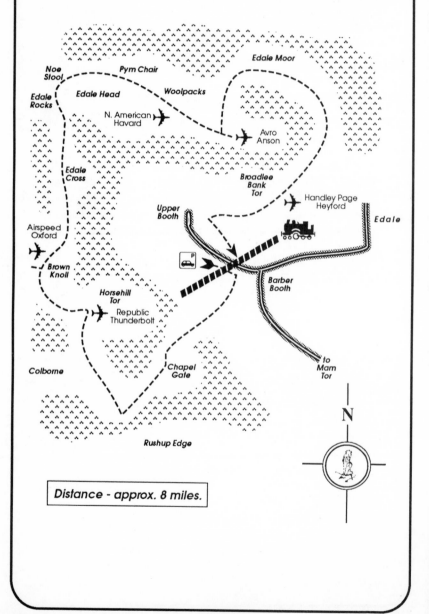

Edale Moor

Noe Stool

Pym Chair

Edale Rocks

Edale Head

Woolpacks

N. American Havard

Avro Anson

Edale Cross

Broadlee Bank Tor

Handley Page Heyford

Edale

Upper Booth

Airspeed Oxford

Brown Knoll

Barber Booth

Horsehill Tor

Republic Thunderbolt

Colborne

Chapel Gate

to Mam Tor

Rushup Edge

N

Distance - approx. 8 miles.

Walk 5
BROWN KNOLL
- allow 6 hours

 - *Car Park above Barber Booth in Vale of Edale*

Grid Reference 107847

👣 👣 *Barber Booth, Chapel Gate, Colborne, Horsehill Tor, Brown Knoll, Trig Point, Swines Back, Noe Stool, The Cloughs, Woolpacks, Crowden Tower, Pennine Way, Grindslow Knoll, Broadlee Bank Tor, Crowden Clough, Upper Booth, Barber Booth.*

WALKING INSTRUCTIONS - Follow the road from the parking area back down to the railway arches, pass beneath them, to a stile situated approx 200 metres further down the road on the right, next to a rickety wooden gate. Cross the stile and follow the track through the fields, crossing a number of stiles and gates, until you reach the wider and rocky track known as 'Chapel Gate', which owes it's name to the fact that in bygone years, it was the main track running from Edale to Chapel-en-le-Frith. Go up the track as it contours the steep flank of 'Lords Seat' on Rushup Edge until you reach a footpath sign and cairn on Colborne Edge, here you leave the track and turn right, heading north-west, along the path that eventually brings you to the summit of Brown Knoll, but before your arrival at the summit, you have a small detour to find the first crash site.

About 15 minutes walking from the cairn will bring you to the remains of a stone sheepfold, just to the right of the track, from here go on a compass bearing of 352° heading northwards, after a few minutes you will reach a memorial cairn and the remains of a wall. The cairn was erected for the National Trust, in memory of John Charles Gilligan, by his family. Cross the stream bed by the cairn and head 72° eastwards for approx 90 metres, where you will find in a small clearing on the slopes of Horsehill Tor, the crash site of the P-47C Thunderbolt. Only a few scraps of molten and twisted metal are left, gathered in a small pile with a few rocks around them to prevent the remains blowing down the hillside.

Return to the cairn and head north-west until you reach the path again, stay on it, if you can, as it becomes rather indistinct at times, and very soggy, climbing up to the summit of Brown Knoll, if you look to your left on the ascent, you should see what appears to be the turret of a castle, it is in fact the air shaft to Cowburn Tunnel, running under Colborne and Toot Hill. On the summit of Brown Knoll you will see a trig point, from here go on a compass bearing of 298° in a westerly direction for approx 210 metres, and in a gully you will find the remains of the Airspeed Oxford. Pieces of twisted and mangled metal, and sections of wood are gathered together in the gully, other fragments are scattered around the area. One of the air crew, (all three survived the crash) was Ted Croker, secretary of the Football Association, he suffered injuries to his ankles, but crawled on hands and knees to Lee House near Upper Booth, to raise the alarm and instigate the rescue of his two crew members, a heroic deed on a bitter winters day.

After your inspection head back to the trig point and follow the path northwards, be prepared to get your boots covered in peat as you sink to your ankles trying to follow the path, keep smiling, the path does improve. After a few minutes you will reach a broken wall with the path running alongside it, follow this until you reach the 'Pennine Way' sign at the foot of 'Swines Back', so named, because from certain angles it is supposed to resemble the back of a pig. To your right is the path down to Jacobs Ladder and Edale, to your left the path to Hayfield. Your way is straight up Swines Back, quite a steep walk, then veer north-west, passing a few large cairns, and Edale Rocks to the left of the path, if you should feel the urge to climb the rocks, go to the rear of them and you will see that they slope gently down to the plateau, so you will have a much easier route to the top of them.

Carry on the path, passing Noe Stool, an anvil shaped rock over looking Edale Head, until you reach the rocky area known as the 'Woolpacks', with the large mass of rocks looking like slabs stacked on top of each other and known as the 'Pagoda', with Pym Chair just off the path to your left. Pym Chair is slightly chair shaped and also has the appearance of two horns sticking out of it, it is supposedly named after John Pym, a minister in the 17th century, who is reputed to have held meetings here.

Walk past the Pagoda for a few metres to a large solitary rock on the right of the path, from here, head on a compass bearing of 156° in a south-east direction, scrambling down the steep grassy slopes of the

'Cloughs' for about 5 minutes, you will then reach a small hollow containing a few scraps of metal and a piece of undercarriage strut from the North American Harvard, now go eastwards for approx 50 metres to a rocky watercourse, scramble down it for 200 metres, and on the right hand bank, in a shallow hollow you will find the rest of the Harvard, sadly, only a few pieces of twisted and mangled metal remain. From here go on a compass bearing of 196° in a southerly direction, down the hillside for approx 150 metres, and in a mossy bog you will find a solitary Cheetah engine from the Avro Anson, no other wreckage remains. The engine is slowly sinking into the boggy hillside, but should remain visible for a long time, maybe at sometime in the near future, a group will be organised to haul the engine out of its watery grave, and set it on firmer ground, as a lasting memorial to the pilot.

Directly below you on the opposite hillside, is the well used Jacobs Ladder path, and no doubt from your lofty position you will see someone struggling up it. It's now time for you to struggle upwards,following the watercourse until you reach the 'Woolpacks'. Here turn right on reaching the path, heading north-east through the rocks, you may wish to spend some time here, marvelling at the strange shapes, some looking like animals, others have faces, and quite a large number look like mushrooms, once through the Woolpacks, you will pass the buttress of Crowden Tower, then the fords over Crowden Clough, here go right, in an easterly direction, you are now on a short section of the Pennine Way, and as you walk along the ridge path, weather permitting, you will have a fine view of the Vale of Edale, and way over to your right the 'Chapel Gate' track where you started from.

After approx 15 minutes you leave the Pennine Way, which goes to your left, carry straight on in a south-east direction along the path to Grindslow Knoll. Take the path that veers right and contours beneath the knoll, stay in a southerly direction, passing two small tarns (that are actually springs) on the left of the path on Broadlee Bank Tor, until you reach a broken wall, turn left just before the wall and walk for about 40 metres to a shallow clearing.This is the crash site of the Handley Page Heyford, only a few rusty struts and pieces of molten and twisted metal are left, as a sad reminder of this fine old aircraft.

After your inspection, go back to the path running through the wall, and scramble down the extremely steep slope of the tor, be very careful if the ground is wet. About two thirds of the way down, the path goes left and right, go right for a few metres to an open country sign, here turn left and go down to a stile, cross this, and another stile a few metres down on the right, then follow the path through the fields in a south-east direction, until you reach a short walled track, at the end of the track, turn left, and at the signpost, go through the wooden gate for Barber Booth, cross the fields and a number of stiles, taking in the magnificent view of the ridges in front of you. As you reach the railway arches, you will see a wooden footbridge crossing the River Noe, cross this, and turn right up the road to your Car Park.

WRECKS SEEN ON THIS WALK -

Republic P47C Thunderbolt 416227
63 Fighter Sqdn USAAF

Crashed on Horsehill Tor 25.4.43
Grid reference- 0935844

Airspeed Oxford HN594/21PAFU   *Crashed on*
Brown Knoll 28.12.45
Grid reference- 082852

North American Harvard FT415
Fleet Air Arm F.T.S.

Crashed Cloughs / Woolpacks 14.1.52
Grid reference- 089868 & 089867

Avro Anson NL185
H.Q. Flight R.A.F. Bomber Command.

Crashed Cloughs / Woolpacks 23.11.45
Grid reference- 0905866

Handley Page Heyford K6875
166 Sqdn

Crashed on
Broadlee Bank Tor 22.7.37
Grid reference- 1095861

Memorial cairn near Thunderbolt crash site - Horsehill Tor - 25.4.43.

Oxford wreckage - Crashed 28.12.45 - Brown Knoll.

WALK 6
EDALE MOOR

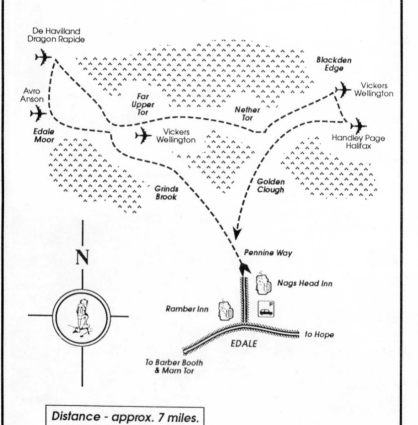

De Havilland
Dragon Rapide

Blackden
Edge

Avro
Anson

Vickers
Wellington

Edale
Moor

Far
Upper
Tor

Nether
Tor

Vickers
Wellington

Handley Page
Halifax

Grinds
Brook

Golden
Clough

N

Pennine Way

Nags Head Inn

Ramber Inn

P

EDALE

to Hope

To Barber Booth
& Mam Tor

Distance - approx. 7 miles.

Walk 6
EDALE MOOR
- allow 5 hours

 - Large Car Park in Edale. Grid reference 124854

•• •• •• - Edale, Grindsbrook Booth, Pennine Way, Edale Moor, Far Upper Tor, Upper Tor, Nether Tor, Blackden Edge Trig Point, Golden Clough, The Nab, Pennine Way, Grindsbrook Booth - Edale

WALKING INSTRUCTIONS - Leave the car park by the toilet block and turn right up the road, passing the Rambler Inn, and Fieldhead Information Centre, where it might pay you to obtain the weather Forecast for the area. Pass the Old Nags Head Inn, and onto the official start (or finish) of the Pennine Way. Cross the wooden footbridge fording Grinds Brook, and up the steps, then through the open pastureland, and trees, to another foot bridge and open country sign. Cross the footbridge and carry straight on. High above you, on your right are the rocky escarpments of 'The Nab' and 'Ringing Roger', the echoing rocks, further up the clough you will see the three rocky buttresses of Nether Tor, Upper Tor and Far Upper Tor, the latter being the tragic crash site of a Wellington Bomber.

High up on the left side of the clough are the rocky areas of Grindslow Knoll and the Fox Holes. The path meanders fairly gently upwards, but as the clough narrows, the path becomes rockier and steeper. You will have to cross the brook a few times to obtain the easiest route up, so care must be taken, as you near the head of the clough the path becomes a mass of rocks and is very steep, guaranteed to warm you up on a cold winters day. The most impressive sight in Grindsbrook is where the stream spills off the moor between the sheer rock walls of Grindsbrook Towers, this rocky cleft on your right is your route out of the clough, instead of the more popular and heavily used Pennine Way running straight up. Scramble up the rocky stream bed running between the Towers, it looks more difficult than it actually is, just take care if the stream is in full flow, there are plenty of dry places on either side to scramble up.

As you reach the head of the cleft, you will see on the left hand side and above you, a large anvil shaped rock, walk up to it and take a compass bearing of 308° and head off in a north-westerly direction across Edale Moor, crossing a few peat gullies as you go. After approx 10 minutes you will come to the remains of an Avro Anson scattered along a shallow gully. There are two 7 cylinder Cheetah engines, wooden and metal sections, and numerous fragments scattered about, some being slowly buried under the peat. After your inspection, set your compass to 12° and head northwards to Wove Hill, with it's small rocky summit, clearly visible on a fine day. It will take you about 10 minutes to reach the crash site at the base of the hill in a rocky area. The remains of the De Havilland Dragon Rapide are piled together and include a six cylinder engine block, some rusty under carriage struts, and metal fragments.

After your investigation, set your compass to 156° and head back to the anvil shaped stone, then onto the ridge path. Head south-east, crossing the brook which runs down to the Towers, and continue along the ridge path. If the weather is kind you will have splendid views of the clough way down below, and no doubt minute figures on their way up. It should take you about 10 minutes to reach the first rocky buttress of 'Far Upper Tor, there you will see a water course running off the moor and through the rocks.

Go past this, to the end of the buttress, and scramble down the slope for about 20 metres, veering right as you go, there you will find the crash site of the Vickers Wellington. Sadly only fragments are left, the twisted and molten pieces are gathered in two small piles, surrounded by rocks to prevent them falling or blowing down the hillside. The area of the impact is barren, the intense heat of the exploding aeroplane rendering it so.

Now climb back up to the ridge path and head eastwards, passing the rocky buttresses of Upper and Nether Tors. It should take you about 20 minutes to reach the head of Golden Clough, with it's large stone cairn a few metres from it's head. At the cairn, set your compass to 54° and head up the slope and onto the moor, heading for the trig point on Blackden Edge, as you move north-easterly up onto the moor, you will see the trig point weather permitting. There is a path of sorts, but you will probably lose it as you cross the peat gullies, 10 minutes should bring you to the soggy peat laden landmark on top of Blackden Edge. Here take a compass bearing of 126° south-east and walk for approx

140 metres, where you will find the pitiful remains of another Wellington on the top of a shallow gully. Just a few fragments of metal are gathered in small pile, although there are other fragments scattered around the area if you wish to explore.

The easiest way to find the next crash site, especially in bad weather, is to go back to the trig point, and go on a compass bearing of 148° south-east, walking for approx 270 metres, there you will find the crash site of the Handley Page Halifax, in a shallow clearing, there is considerably more of this than the Wellington. You will find a sheet of armour plating, reinforcing struts and numerous pieces of metal piled together. After your inspection turn your thoughts to the way back to the car park in Edale. You can return either by going back to Grindsbrook, or passing Ringing Roger and going down by the 'Nab', or the route I prefer, it is less popular but quite a nice way down. Return to the trig point, and set your compass to 234° west, ten minutes walking will bring you to just below the head of Golden Clough, not far from the large cairn.

Follow the rocky path down the left hand side of the stream bed, passing through a large area of fern, the path then veers in two directions, to the left, and straight ahead, this is your route, staying on the left of the stream bed, until you reach the trees and footbridge at the bottom of the clough. Go through the wooden gate, and along the path through the trees, then through another wooden gate and along a short stretch of Pennine Way, until you reach the road in Edale, and so back to your car park.

Anson - engine wreckage - crashed 11.12.44.- Edale Moor.

WRECKS SEEN ON THIS WALK -

Avro Anson N.9853-16SFTS   Crashed Edale Moor 11.12.44
                                                  Grid reference- 101878

De Havilland Dragon Rapide G-ALBC
of Solair Flying Services   Crashed Edale Moor 30.12.63
                                                  Grid reference- 102883

Vickers Wellington W5719
150 Sqdn   Crashed Far Upper Tor 31.7.41
                                                  Grid reference- 1118755

Vickers Wellington X3348
427 Sqdn   Crashed Blackden Edge 26.1.43
                                                  Grid reference- 13058775

Handley Page Halifax HR727
51 Sqdn   Crashed Blackden Edge 5.10.43
                                                  Grid reference- 131876

Wellington remains - crashed 31.7.41. - below Far Upper Tor.

Halifax wreckage - crashed 5.10.43. - near Trig Point on Blackden Edge.

Dragon Rapide wreckage - crashed 30.12.63 - Wove Hill, Edale Moor.

WALK 7
MILL HILL

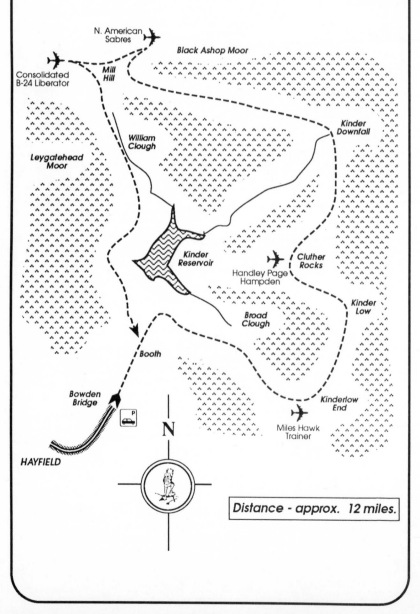

N. American Sabres

Black Ashop Moor

Mill Hill

Consolidated B-24 Liberator

Kinder Downfall

William Clough

Leygatehead Moor

Kinder Reservoir

Cluther Rocks

Handley Page Hampden

Kinder Low

Broad Clough

Booth

Bowden Bridge

Kinderlow End

Miles Hawk Trainer

HAYFIELD

N

Distance - approx. 12 miles.

Walk 7
MILL HILL
- allow 6 to 7 hours.

 - *Car Park at Bowden Bridge Quarry Grid reference 048869*

•• •• •• - *Bowden Bridge, Kinder Road, Booth, Hill House Estate, Kinder Low End, Kinder Low, Trig Point, Cluther Rocks, Pennine Way, Kinder Downfall, Pennine Way, Ashop Head, Black Ashop Moor, Mill Hill, William Clough, Kinder Reservoir, Kinder Road, Bowden Bridge.*

***WALKING NOTES - *** *The car park was an old quarry and is featured in the mass trespass onto Kinder in 1932. There is a memorial plaque on the quarry wall.*

WALKING INSTRUCTIONS - From the car park turn left up the road and at the metal gates of the N.W.W. about 1/2 mile away, turn right crossing the bridge over the River Kinder following the footpath sign, staying on the tarmaced road as it veers right to Booth, here follow the Public Bridleway sign going straight ahead through the hamlet of Booth. The road follows a walled lane through the trees until you reach an Open Country sign on the right, here go through the wooden gate on the Hill House Estate, following the path up to the trees, to a stile and metal gate, cross the stile and turn right up the track to another gate and stile. Cross these and go up the hill following the fence line, here you have a magnificent view of the western flanks of the Kinder Plateau, and if the prevailing wind is westerly, as it often is, you should see the spray from the Kinder Downfall spiralling upwards from the rocky ravine, a quite exceptional sight in the High Peak.

Follow the path until you reach a broken wall, then follow the wall keeping it on your left, and as the wall veers to the left, carry on straight ahead passing through a gap in the next wall. The path meanders through open pastureland, until you reach a gate and stile and an Open Country sign. Cross the stile and turn right following the walled track, keeping the wall on your right until you reach a wooden gate and stile. Do not cross the stile, turn left in an easterly direction and scramble up the steep rocky track to the summit of Kinderlow End. Carry on along the ridge path easterly, passing above the crash site of a Miles Hawk Trainer. The remains of the aircraft were buried at the crash site, which is situated between the ridge path and the lower path, contouring beneath Kinder Low. I have searched unsuccessfully for the site, maybe you will have better luck if you decide to go exploring. The ridge path eventually veers to the left, following a fence, about 150 metres from the rocky buttress of Edale Rocks, and meanders up to a large cairn and trig point on Kinder Low.

From the trig point take a compass reading of 352° north, crossing the rocks and peaty area of Kinder Low, it will take you a few minutes to reach the crash site of the Hampden Bomber on Cluther Rocks. The majority of the small remnants are piled together just below a large mass of rocks, there are pieces of molten metal and rusty nuts and bolts. The area is covered in tiny fragments scattered about the rocks, I quite often spend a few minutes searching between the rocks unearthing more fragments. From your lofty vantage point you have a splendid view of Kinder Reservoir. After your inspection, continue along the path northwards to the Downfall. This path being the Pennine Way Alternative Route, easily discernible by the stone cairns waymarking the route.

Crossing the great buttress and the River Kinder at the head of the Downfall, you will probably decide to stop and rest awhile and take in the magnificent view from here, as thousands of people do the whole year round. If you decide to eat here, the sheep will soon be milling around you, quite happy to eat as much of your food as possible, they will attack your rucksack if given the chance, so be warned. Carry on along the Pennine Way, it has become badly eroded in places and rather vague, though a number of cairns mark the route, on a clear day the scenery is spectacular and the walk rewarding, but in adverse weather it becomes a hard slog. You will pass above Kinder Buttress and Sandy Heys, then the Upper Western Buttress and eventually reaching Mill Hill Rocks at Ashop Head. From the cairns take a compass bearing of 120° south east, and head up the gentle slope for a few hundred metres, passing a number of rocky outcrops. A few minutes walking will bring you to a flat area on the Kinder plateau, not far from a prominent rocky knoll. There on a peat bed, you will find numerous small pieces from the wrecked Sabres, and in shallow gullies nearby. A lot of the wreckage has stencilled lettering, still quite legible. The whole area is well worth exploring, especially The Gullies, as the wreckage tends to collect in them, no doubt blown there by the atrocious winds on Kinder. After your exploration of the area, head north to the slopes running down to Black Ashop Moor. If the weather is fine, you will see the main bulk of the wrecked Sabres far below. The way down is quite steep, so care should be taken.

The wreckage covers quite a large area and includes two wheels and undercarriage legs. Large sections of wing numbered XD 707 and XD 730 and numerous other parts, some quite large, scattered around the area. There are more fragments higher up the slopes near Ashop Head. The Sabres are reputed to have collided in mid-air, so fragments will have scattered over a very large area. I have found pieces very close to Ashop Head and a colleague found a large section near the edge path, so if you feel adventurous and the weather is fine, you may find it very rewarding to explore the area. At the site is a memorial plaque in remembrance of the two pilots, FLT. LT. GREEN and F.0. HORNE, laid by the cadets of 1890 DET.FLT.A.T.C.

Above you to the south is the Kinder Edge, with it's abundance of rocky features of which the Boxing Glove Stones can be seen. Now set your compass to 288° west and head up the moor towards Mill Hill, keeping Ashop Head on your left, crossing the grassy and sometimes marshy ground up the slopes of Mill Hill, eventually reaching a wooden post on it's summit. Here take a compass reading of 318° north west and head down the slope, there is a faint path which you can follow to the next crash site, but at times it becomes rather vague. If you stay on your compass bearing, you will reach the crash site of the Liberator in about 5 minutes. There are two 14 cylinder radial engines, large sections of undercarriage, a large section of wing and sheets of armour plating and other parts in gullies around the area. The site is reputed to be haunted, but up to now I have seen no ghostly figures, maybe you will have the pleasure. Now head 260° west for approx 100 metres, and in a large gully you will find both wings and an engine from the Liberator. Further scrambling around the surrounding gullies will reveal more pieces of wreckage, some partly buried by the clinging peat. After your exploration, go back to the main crash site, and from there head back to the summit of Mill Hill on a bearing of 138° south east, and pick up the Pennine Way at the wooden post and head south down the soggy peat path to a wooden signpost at the foot of Ashop Head. Here turn right for Hayfield, going down William Clough, named after William The Smith, a miner in medieval times who worked near the clough.

The path is badly eroded in places so care must be taken, you will need to cross the stream a number of times, to obtain the easiest and safest route down. At the bottom of the clough, follow the path that runs along the right hand side of Kinder Reservoir. Taking in the splendid views on your left of the ridge walk you have just completed. The path eventually runs between two walls which end at a gate and tarmaced road, here turn left following the footpath sign, crossing a footbridge, then veering right taking the path running through the trees and accompanying the River Kinder, until you reach the road leading back to your car park.

WRECKS SEEN ON THIS WALK -

Miles Hawk Trainer G-AJSF   Crashed Kinder Low End 28.7.57
(no trace)   Grid reference - 074868

Handley Page Hampden A.E. 381
                     Crashed Cluther Rocks 21.1.42
                     Grid reference - 078875

North American FL86 Sabres   Crashed Black Ashop Moor
XD 707 & XD 730 66 Sqdn.   22.7.54
         Grid reference - 072902 & 071897

Consolidated B-24 Liberator   Crashed Mill Hill 10.11.44
42-52003 U.S.A.A.F.
310 Ferrying Sqdn.   Grid reference - 058907 & 057907

Hampden wreckage
- crashed 21.1.42 -
Cluther Rocks.

B-24 Liberator - main undercarriage wheel - crashed 10.11.44 - Mill Hill.

Sabres wreckage - crashed 22.7.54. - Black Ashop Moor.

WALK 8
TINTWISTLE KNARR

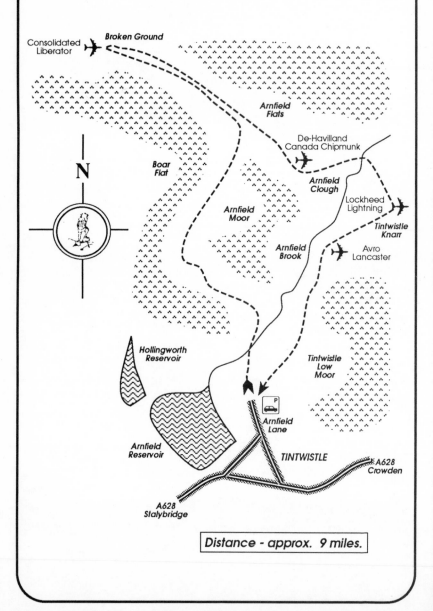

Consolidated Liberator

Broken Ground

Arnfield Flats

De-Havilland Canada Chipmunk

Boar Flat

Arnfield Clough

Lockheed Lightning

Arnfield Moor

Tintwistle Knarr

Arnfield Brook

Avro Lancaster

Hollingworth Reservoir

Tintwistle Low Moor

Arnfield Reservoir

Arnfield Lane

TINTWISTLE

A628 Crowden

A628 Stalybridge

Distance - approx. 9 miles.

Walk 8
TINTWISTLE KNARR
- allow 6 to 7 hours

🚗 P *At the top of Arnfield Lane. The lane is situated in Tintwistle off the A628, just above Arnfield Reservoir. Grid reference 017980*

👣 👣 👣 - *Arnfield Lane, Ogden Clough, Bowerclough Head, Broken Ground, Bowerclough Head, Arnfield Flats, Arnfield Clough, Tintwistle Knarr, Arnfield Brook, Arnfield Lane.*

WALKING NOTES - *The PB4Y-1 Liberator on Broken Ground is on private land owned by The Stalybridge Estates; from whom permission should be requested before entering their land.*

WALKING INSTRUCTIONS - From the parking area, proceed up the walled lane northwards to a wooden gate and stile, with an open country sign. Cross these and carry straight on, then where the track veers left and right , go left in a northerly direction, following the stone wall, catching glimpses of Arnfield Reservoir over the wall. The track meanders to the left and right, gradually winding downhill, passing a wall stile which you ignore. The track eventually reaches a stile and footbridge crossing Ogden Brook. Cross the footbridge, and veer left following the footpath sign, the path then goes uphill, following a stone wall, until you reach the 'Footpath to Chew Valley' signpost. Follow the signposted way, turning right east wards. The path is waymarked with small stone cairns and a few posts. About half an hours walking will bring you to another Open Country sign, and wooden footbridge crossing Ogden Brook. Cross the bridge and leave the path, following the fence on your left for approx 2 miles, although you are off the beaten track, the way is fairly easy.

Where the fence comes to a sudden end at Bowerclough Head, just below Chew Hurdles, take a compass bearing of 298° and head westerly across Irontongue Hill, crossing a number of watercourses and peat gullies. The going is rather strenuous in places, but not too difficult, about thirty minutes walking will bring you to a large expanse of flat peatland on 'Broken Ground'. Here you will find the crash site of the Consolidated PB4Y-1 Liberator. A fair amount of wreckage is strewn over a large area. There are sheets of rusty armour plating, undercarriage struts and legs, two 14 cylinder radial engines, and pieces of twisted metal scattered around the area.

After your inspection (and rest), retrace your steps back to the fence at Bowerclough Head on 118° easterly. On reaching the end of the fence, set your compass to 162° and head south, to the staked enclosures above the shooting cabins on Arnfield Moor. It should take you approx 30 minutes to reach your destination, crossing the rock strewn mass of Arnfield Flats. On reaching the enclosures, proceed from the left hand one (which looks as though it was some kind of weather station, in years gone by) on a compass reading of 294° , and walk westerly for approx 375 metres, you will pass a large wooden post on your compass reading, the crash site is about 100 metres below this in a rock and peaty area. Sadly, only a few pieces of twisted metal from the De Havilland Canada Chipmunk are left, gathered into a small pile. There are a lot of tiny fragments embedded in the peat, you may find other pieces if you scout around the area. After your exploration, head back to the enclosures on 114° easterly. From them, head east-wards up to the head of Arnfield Clough, keeping to it's left flank, you will cross a number of rocky watercourses with some heather and peat expanses, which can be hard going in wet weather.

As you near the head of the clough, follow the path until you reach the first watercourse running in from the left, just before Arnfield Brook starts to zig zag. From here, cross the brook and head on a compass bearing of 204° southerly, to the corner of the fencing on the top of Tintwistle Knarr, which you will see on a clear day. On reaching the fence corner (it has a Ministry of Agriculture sign post next to it) go on a compass bearing of 162° southerly, heading across Tintwistle Knarr. About 10 minutes hard walking over peaty and boggy ground, will bring you to the crash site of the P38J Lightning. It lies more or less between two wooden marker posts, approx 100 metres from the fencing, running alongside the path above the reservoirs. The remains of the Lightning are in three small clearings within a few metres of each other in the heather. All the pieces are piled together, they are all twisted and molten lumps of metal, a sorry epitaph to a famous American Fighter Plane.

After your inspection, head north westerly up the hill side to the fencing on top of Tintwistle Knarr. You will find a stile crossing the top section of fencing, cross the stile, and go down hill south westerly, following a large rocky Watercourse. About 150 metres down you will find the crash site of the Avro Lancaster. There are a number of rusty undercarriage legs and struts, pieces of armour plating, engine cogs, and pieces of twisted and molten metal scattered around the area, sadly, these are all that remain of this once mighty bomber.

After you inspection, carry on down hill, until you reach the bottom stile crossing the fence, cross the stile and head down the hillside in a westerly direction, towards the lower reaches of Arnfield Clough, keeping the brook on your right. A ten minute scramble through the heather, will bring you to a sunken path which you follow, keeping a line of grouse butts to your left, eventually, reaching a wider grassy track which you follow to a metal gate and stile. Cross these, and another stile approx 1/4 mile further along the track, then pass the cottages on your left, and turn right on reaching Arnfield Lane. Cross the stone bridge and walk up to your parking area.

WRECKS SEEN ON THIS WALK -

Consolidated PB4Y-1 *Liberator 63934* *VB110 Bombing Sqdn. U.S.N.*	*Crashed Broken Ground 18.12.43* *Grid reference - 006018*
De-Havilland Canada *Chipmunk WB579 No 2 R.F.S*	*Crashed Arnfield Moor 3.7.51* *Grid reference - 0279975*
Avro Lancaster *PA411/A3-U230 OCU.*	*Crashed Tintwistle Knarr* *21.12.48* *Grid reference - 034993*
Lockheed P38J Lightning *42 - 67207 H Q Sqdn.* *554 F.T.S. 496 Fighter* *Training Group U.S.A.A.F.*	*Crashed Tintwistle Knarr* *10.5.44* *Grid reference - 039992*

P38J Lightning wreckage - crashed 10.5.44 - Tintwistle Knarr.

Lancaster undercarraige struts - crashed 21.12.48 - Tintwistle Knarr.

Liberator - main undercarriage - crashed 19.12.43. - Broken Ground.

Liberator - engine - crashed 19.12.43. - Broken Ground.

WALK 9
MARGERY HILL

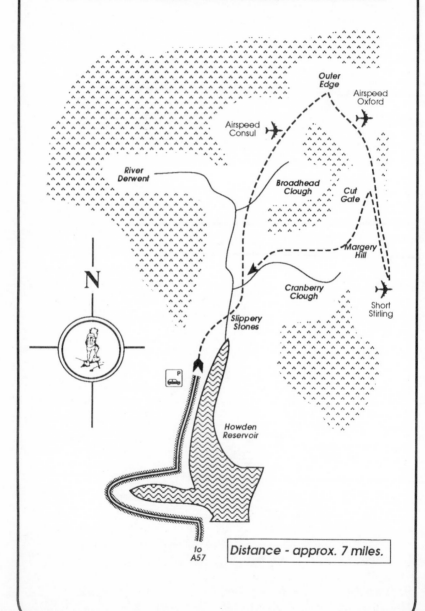

Outer Edge

Airspeed Oxford

Airspeed Consul

River Derwent

Broadhead Clough

Cut Gate

Margery Hill

Cranberry Clough

Short Stirling

Slippery Stones

N

P

Howden Reservoir

to A57

Distance - approx. 7 miles.

Walk 9
MARGERY HILL
- allow 5 to 6 hours.

Parking At the Kings Tree, where the road ends at the northern (upper) reaches of Howden Reservoir. Grid reference 16759385

•● ●● •● - *Howden Reservoir, Slippery Stones, Cranberry Bed, Broadhead Clough, Outer Edge, Trig Point, Margery Hill, Trig Point, Stainery Clough, Margery Hill, Cut Gate, Little Cut, Quarries (Disused) Slippery Stones, Howden Reservoir.*

WALKING NOTES - *The road to Kings Tree from Fairholmes has vehicular access restrictions, these operate over Bank Holidays and weekends, from April till the end of October. At such times, a minibus service operates from Fairholmes to Kings Tree, so be sure to check on the timetables, as not to miss the bus back, at the end of your walk, the distance back to Fairholmes from Kings Tree being nearly five miles.*

The Short Stirling near Stainery Clough is on private land owned by Wilsons, whose land is maintained by the gamekeeper, Mr.D.Taylor Ewden Lodge Farm, Mortimer Road, Boltsterstones; from whom permission should be requested before entering their land.

WALKING INSTRUCTIONS - From the parking area, pass through the wooden gate and walk northerly along the track adjacent to the reservoir, crossing the stepping stones, where Linch Clough's waters pour into the reservoir. The track meanders through a wooded area, much frequented by Ornithologists, as you will no doubt see for yourself, I have watched them on numerous occasions as they scan the trees with their binoculars and telescopes. The track eventually reaches a fine 17th century packhorse bridge at Slippery Stones, re-sited here in 1959, owing to the submerging of Derwent Village. After crossing the bridge, veer left, passing some old wooden sheep pens, until you reach the Fred Heardman Memorial footbridge on the Derwent Estate. Turn right after crossing the bridge, and follow the track northerly, passing the entrance to Cranberry Clough on your right, with the Howden Moor N.T. sign. Carry on, keeping company with Cranberry

Bed on your left, with Swineside and the hump of Little Moor on your right. A few minutes walking will bring you to a grassy rising track on the right, leading up to Broadhead Clough, follow this to a N.T. sign depicting a woodland conservation area which is fenced off. Follow the fence line until you reach a small wooden footbridge, fording the watercourse running down Broadhead Clough.

Cross the bridge and turn right, keeping to the left side of the watercourse, steadily climbing upwards. Gradually, veer to the left, keeping north easterly until you pick up the line of grouse butts (be sure that you follow the left hand line of butts running up the clough, another line also runs up the right hand side of the clough.) Keep climbing upwards north easterly, the going is quite strenuous, also beware of numerous knee deep holes, which are likely to be full of water, as I have found to my cost a fair number of times. The line of butts do not run in an orthodox line, but if you travel north easterly, you will eventually reach the crash site which is situated close to number two butt. Just to the right of the butt in a rocky watercourse, you will find a Cheetah engine and numerous pieces of metal and wiring, from the Airspeed Consul, while above the butt, in a flat peaty clearing you will find more pieces of metal and wood, with wiring and pieces of fuel pipes.

If you decide to explore the area, you will no doubt come across more fragments in the peat and heather, though the largest sections are in the watercourse. After your inspection, go on a compass bearing of 46°, heading north easterly, crossing an expanse of tufted grass and heather, up to the trig point which is situated above the rocky outcrop of Outer Edge. It should take about ten minutes to reach the trig point, from there, follow the fairly well defined path south easterly for approx 500 metres. The path can be one long sodden trek which isn't very enjoyable, especially after prolonged rain, so good footwear is needed. The path is waymarked with small wooden posts, at the 8th post from the trig point, (500 metres) turn left off the path for approx 35 metres, and in a long peat gully, you will find the remains of the Airspeed Oxford, there are small sections of wood, and numerous pieces of twisted metal scattered along the gully, also near the 8th post, you will find more small fragments embedded in a flat peat bed. After your inspection of the site, carry on along the path south easterly, towards the trig point on Margery Hill. You will have to traverse a number of peat gullies, which may throw you off the path on occasions. Eventually you will reach a stone cairn at the junction of your path and the Cut Gate Track, carry on south easterly for a few minutes, until you reach the flat rocky top of Margery Hill, on which the trig point stands.

From there, go on a compass bearing of 114° , heading easterly, towards Stainery Clough, you will cross a large expanse of heather moorland, with watercourses and peat gullies to scramble up and down. If the weather is kind, you will see a large chimney on the horizon, I find this a good guide, and you should keep it more or less straight in front of you on your compass bearing. About 25 minutes hard walking will bring you to the crash site of the Short Stirling. There are masses of wreckage scattered over a large area, in a long peat gully, you will find sections of wing and fuselage, engine casings, armour plating, and numerous pieces from the shattered bomber. About 50 metres to the left of the gully, you will find more wreckage strewn down the heather slope, for at least 100 metres, including more sections of wing and fuselage, undercarriage, including a leg with the wheel still intact, although some mindless person has been hacking at the tyre. The whole area is well worth exploring, with many smaller pieces hidden amongst the heather.

After your inspection, head back up the hillside on 298° north westerly to the trig point on Margery Hill, it's a hard slog, but well worth the effort, and the views of the surrounding moorland and hills are quite magnificent. The large rocks at Margery Stones are a good windbreak and an ideal resting place. From the trig point, follow the path back to the cairn, which you passed earlier at the Cut Gate junction. From the cairn, turn left, and follow the wide grassy rock strewn track down past Cut Gate End and Little Cut. The striking rocky buttress over to your right are the Bull Stones, near the head of Bull Clough. The track gradually meanders down to the stream where Cranberry and Bull Cloughs meet, just below some old quarry workings.

Cross the stream and carry on along the track westerly, keeping the stream on your left, passing the Bamford and Flouch Inn footpath sign, and crossing the stream at the Fred Heardman footbridge, then again at the packhorse bridge at Slippery Stones, you now follow your starting path back to the parking area at the Kings Tree.

WRECKS SEEN ON THIS WALK -

Airspeed Consul TF - RPM.

*Crashed below Outer Edge
12. 5.51
Grid reference - 17459665*

Airspeed Oxford LX 518

*Crashed near Margery Hill
19.10.43
Grid reference - 181967*

Short Stirling LJ 628
1654 Heavy Conversion
Unit.

*Crashed near Stainery Clough
Upper Commons 21. 7.44
Grid reference - 1989535*

Oxford LX518 wreckage - crashed 19.10.43. - Margery Hill.

Consul wreckage - crashed 12.5.51. - below Outer Edge.

Stirling wreckage - crashed 21.7.44. - near Stainery Clough.

WALK RECORD CHART

Date walked

WALK 1 - DOVESTONES & CHEW AREA ....

WALK 2 - HOLME MOSS ....

WALK 3 - HIGHER SHELF STONES ....

WALK 4 - ROUND HILL ....

WALK 5 - BROWN KNOLL ....

WALK 6 - EDALE MOOR ....

WALK 7 - MILL HILL ....

WALK 8 - TINTWISTLE KNARR ....

WALK 9 - MARGERY HILL ....

GET A JOHN MERRILL LONG WALK BADGE - Complete six of these walks and send a copy of the Walk Record Chart and £2.50 payable to JNM PUBLICATIONS for a signed certificate and badge - 3 1/2 diameter and four colour embroidered on a blue cloth.

"I'VE GONE A JOHN MERRILL WALK" T SHIRT - £6.50 - all sizes - emerald green with white lettering.
J.N.M. Publications, Winster, Matlock, Derbys. DE4 2DQ

************** you may photocopy this page **************

A FEW NOTES ON WALKING IN THE HIGH COUNTRY

Walking should be a pleasurable experience and all the walks in this book are geared to ensure maximum enjoyment. They are circular, through diverse scenery and have much of interest to see on the way. To get even better enjoyment the following are a few guidelines.

Blisters: Always ensure that your boots are comfortable and broken in. Your socks should be close fitting and have no kinks in them. Blisters happen without warning and are a 'fact of life'. If you get one, cover the area well with moleskin or second skin and ensure that your boots are laced reasonably tight. Don't prick them as this can cause infection or for the skin to rub off which is even more harmful.

Walking clothing: Wear a shirt, pullover and windjacket as a basic rule with either corduroy trousers or walking breeches. Do not wear jeans as these can be a death trap if conditions worsen. In winter a duvet or a thinsulate jacket will keep you warm in the coldest weather. Gloves and hat are also a must. In the summer a pair of shorts is quite adequate.

Emergency: Carry a whistle and torch and know the International Distress Signal of six blasts in a minute with a minute silence between. The reply is three blasts in a minute with a minute silence between. If you have to alert the police give them full details and a grid reference of where the injured person is. It is also useful to carry a bar of Kendal mint cake or some chocolate.

Walking speed: There is no need to rush when walking, a pleasant steady pace is all that is required. As a basic rule an average person will walk 2 1/2 to 3 miles in one hour or ascend 2,000 feet in one hour. When climbing uphill adopt a slow, steady pace and keep it up. Descending you can relax and quicken your pace.

Some good advice here.

NATURAL HISTORY NOTES

The moorland areas of Kinder and Bleaklow are fascinating places and have several special features. The following are some of them.

 FLORA:

Peat: Kinder and Bleaklow provide ideal locations for peat to form; the fact that they are waterlogged means that bacterial activity cannot break down the dead plant remains. The peat began forming 7,500 years ago from sphagnum moss. When this plant dies the next growth appears on top forming the very thick surface we see today. The surface vegetation is mostly cotton grass, bilberry and cloudberry and is a result of man's influence by draining and burning the area. Burning has been carried out for many centuries and some charcoal found in the peat has been carbon dated to 1300 A.D. Sphagnum moss, because of its absorbent qualities, was used during World War I in hospitals as a surgical dressing. From pollen grains taken from the peat it has been possible to record chronologically the vegetational history of the area:

> **9,000B .C.**—Only trees such as rowan, willow and juniper existed.
> **8,200 B.C.**—Warmer climate. Birch, juniper and pine growing.
> **7,600 B.C.**—Warmer with oak, elm and hazel trees growing.
> **5,600 B.C.**—Decline in tree pollen. The climate warmer and drier and peat growth stationary.
> **600 B.C.**—Climate like today's—cooler and wetter. Peat grew rapidly. Drainage channels began to form.

Cotton Grass: White hairy heads that wave in the breeze are seen in May and June. Common cotton grass has five or six heads at the top of each stem. Hair's Tail cotton grass has only one head.

Cloudberry: Usually grows above 2,000 ft. Has kidney-shaped leaves and the stems mainly spread underground. The flowers appear in midsummer and both male and female plants have their own flower. The fruit is edible and like a yellow raspberry.

Bilberry: Sometimes known as whortleberry. The shrub grows to about two feet tall and has green bell-shaped leaves. The round blue-

-black berries appear in July.

Juniper: Can be seen growing in several areas. Instead of being upright the branches spread along the ground. The actual trunk can be quite thick.

 # BIRDS:

Red Grouse: Native and unique to Britain. Grows to about 15 inches and has a red/brown body with dark wings and tail. Lives largely on ling heather. The nest is usually a scrape in the ground lined with heather or grass. The female lays between four and nine eggs in April or May. The eggs are white with dark blotches.

Curlew: Often seen and heard on the moors during the summer. It is at twenty-two inches our largest wader and has a long curving beak. Nests on the moor and lines its nest with grass or heather. Usually four eggs are laid, brown with dark blotches.

Ring Ouzel: Visitor to Britain during the summer months and about the same size as a thrush. Black in colour with a white 'bib' on the breast. They can often be seen singing from a rock. Their diet is both animal and vegetable food.

MOUNTAIN HARE: Often known as blue hares as their fur has a bluish appearance in spring and autumn. Although often seen during the summer months, they come into their own in winter and are easily recognised. Their coats turn white and only their ear tips remain black. They are very conspicuous in winter for there are very few days when snow is actually lying on the moors.

SUGGESTED FURTHER READING

High Peak by Eric Byne and Geoffrey Sutton. Secker & Warburg,

Dark Peak Wrecks by Ron Collier and Ron Wilkinson. Barnsley Chronicle, 1979. (Two volumes).

High Ground Wrecks by David J. Smith. Midland Counties Publications, 1989.

Freedom to Roam by Howard Hill. Moorland Publishing Ltd., 1980.

Rock Climbing Guides to Kinder, Bleaklow, Laddow, Chew and Saddleworth Moors.

Circular Walks on Kinder and Bleaklow by John N. Merrill. JNM Publications, 1990.

☆✯☆✯☆✯☆✯

Heyford wreckage - crashed 22.7.37. - Broadlee Bank Tor. - Walk No. 5.

EQUIPMENT NOTES
.... some personal thoughts

BOOTS - *preferably with a full leather upper, of medium weight, with a vibram sole. I always add a foam cushioned insole to help cushion the base of my feet.*

SOCKS - *I generally wear two thick pairs as this helps minimise blisters. The inner pair are of loop stitch variety and approximately 80% wool. The outer are a thick rib pair of approximately 80% wool.*

WATERPROOFS - *for general walking I wear a T shirt or cotton shirt with a cotton wind jacket on top. You generate heat as you walk and I prefer to layer my clothes to avoid getting too hot. Depending on the season will dictate how many layers you wear. In soft rain I just use my wind jacket for I know it quickly dries out. In heavy or consistant rain I slip on a neoprene lined gagoule, and although hot and clammy it does keep me reasonably dry. Only in extreme conditions will I don overtrousers, much preferring to get wet and feel comfortable. I never wear gaiters!*

FOOD - *as I walk I carry bars of chocolate, for they provide instant energy and are light to carry. In winter a flask of hot coffee is welcome. I never carry water and find no hardship from not doing so, but this is a personal matter! From experience I find the more I drink the more I want and sweat. You should always carry some extra food such as Kendal Mint Cake, for emergencies.*

RUCKSACKS - *for day walking I use a climbing rucksack of about 40 litre capacity and although it leaves excess space it does mean that the sac is well padded, with an internal frame and padded shoulder straps. Inside apart from the basics for one day I carry gloves, balaclava, spare pullover and a pair of socks.*

MAP & COMPASS - *when I am walking I always have the relevant map - preferably 1:25,000 scale - open in my hand. This enables me to constantly check that I am walking the right way. In case of bad weather I carry a compass, which once mastered gives you complete confidence in thick cloud or mist.*